Original title:
Life: Still Waiting for Clarity

Copyright © 2025 Creative Arts Management OÜ
All rights reserved.

Author: Cassandra Whitaker
ISBN HARDBACK: 978-1-80566-235-8
ISBN PAPERBACK: 978-1-80566-530-4

The Weight of Unspoken Thoughts

In my head, a dance of dreams,
Thoughts float like tangled seams,
Jokes I ponder, laughter lost,
I laugh alone, at what it costs.

When I trip on what to say,
Words escape in disarray,
My mind's a circus, thoughts collide,
In silence, chuckles try to hide.

When Questions Surfaced

Why is the sky not purple today?
Where do missing socks go astray?
Is the fridge a portal to the stars?
I ponder oddities, with coffee in jars.

Are cats truly the rulers of all?
Do trees giggle when they fall?
These mysteries twist my head just right,
As I chuckle at the cosmic plight.

In the Absence of Answers

I flipped a coin for my career,
Heads I win, tails I fear!
But the quarter rolls away from me,
Just like my plans, who can agree?

Why do we follow paths unclear?
Hoping each twist will bring us cheer,
I misplaced my map and wandered off,
Can someone bring me back, or just scoff?

Tangled in Tomorrow's Tapestry

I weave the future with threads of doubt,
Stitching dreams while in and out,
A pattern formed from joy and fright,
Riddled with snags, it's quite a sight.

Will tomorrow bring pie or cake?
Or will I just end up in a lake?
I laugh at yesterday's silly plans,
Unraveled yarn lies in my hands.

Searching Shadows

In a world of tangled thoughts,
I chase the shadows of my socks.
They dance like whispers on the floor,
And giggle at my endless blocks.

Questions pop like bubblegum,
What's underneath the toaster, please?
I peek but find the crumbs of fun,
With dust bunnies plotting to tease.

In Quest of Hidden Pages

I search for wisdom in my books,
But find only coffee stains instead.
The pages turn like secret looks,
That mock my thoughts and leave me fled.

Between the lines, the jokes are sly,
A riddle wrapped in comic strips.
Each chapter's high, then low, then why,
Like dodging raindrops in tight grips.

A Symphony of Unanswered Whys

The orchestra plays with silly tunes,
Questions fly like kites in air.
The conductor's lost among the moons,
And shrugs as if he didn't care.

I wave my hands, a tune to share,
But all I get is silent notes.
The harmony's a little bare,
With laughter bubbling in my coats.

Brushes with Uncertainty

I paint my days with colors bright,
But find I've used the wrong mix.
A canvas full of sheer delight,
Turns into splatters and wild tricks.

With every stroke, I laugh and sigh,
A masterpiece of happy blunders.
Though clarity's forever shy,
My paintbrush plays while thunder thunders.

Searching for Illumination

In the fridge, I seek the truth,
A yogurt cup that's past its youth.
The light is dim, the choices few,
  For wisdom hid in cereal too.

Like socks that vanish, oh so sly,
Where do they go? I aim to pry.
A fortune cookie said 'Just wait!'
  For clarity on my dinner plate.

Flickers of Distant Light

I squint into the glowing screen,
Seeking answers, barely seen.
A meme recalls a distant star,
My life's so bright, yet feels bizarre.

Are those dreams or just my snacks?
Where's the road? I lost the maps!
Warning signs fly past my mind,
I'll trip on wisdom, never find.

A Labyrinth of Dreams

Through buttered toast, my thoughts collide,
An endless maze I can't abide.
The paths are twisted, all around,
Where's the exit? Not a sound!

I chase my shadow, what a game,
He's laughing loud, I feel the shame.
With every turn, I meet the paste,
Wisdom's buried with my breakfast haste.

Threads of Time

They say I'm woven with the past,
But hold on tight, this yarn won't last.
I knit with hope, a tangled mess,
Yet laugh at all my happy stress.

Oh, clock, stop spinning, take a break,
Let's make mistakes, for goodness' sake!
Each tick resounds, a silly chime,
In fabric soft, I lose all rhyme.

The Puzzle of Perpetual Inquiry

Lost my keys in the couch, what a feat,
Maybe they're dancing, quite the treat.
Questions whirl, like bees in a hive,
Should I get up, or just stay and thrive?

Thoughts like socks, they wander far,
Hoping to find my inner star.
Puzzles piled high, oh what a mess,
Could clarity be hiding in my stress?

Jigsaw pieces, none fit right,
Yet here I am, it's quite the sight.
The answers laugh, they play a game,
Who knew inquiry was such a name!

Oh what joy to chase each clue,
With laughter ringing, bright and true.
Maybe the point is to just enjoy,
The maze of questions, oh what a ploy!

Dancing with Doubt

Waltz with worry, oh what a dance,
Twirl in confusion, give it a chance.
Do I step left, or right with grace?
The mirror reflects a question's face.

Clumsy partner, this doubt of mine,
Stomping on toes, but feeling fine.
Laughing at missteps, we both fall,
Maybe it's fun; I'll just give it my all.

Shall we tango with uncertainty,
Each step a giggle, a chance to be free?
Caught in a spin, but I can't complain,
As laughter echoes through joy and pain.

Round and round in this funny maze,
Ballet of questions igniting a blaze.
But I'll keep dancing, toes raw and sore,
With a smile that says, I'm always wanting more!

Fragments Yet to Be

Scattered pieces lie on the floor,
Each one's a story, that's for sure.
Collecting fragments, what a treat,
Can't quite grasp them, oh isn't that neat?

Colorful shapes whisper and tease,
"Look at us, will you please?"
Trying to build with what I know,
Yet every effort ends up in a throw.

Crafting my tale from bits and ends,
Dreams in a box that never bends.
I laugh as I search for sense and rhyme,
Knowing well, all things take time.

So gather the scraps, make a parade,
The humor in chaos will never fade.
With every piece I twirl and spin,
Maybe the puzzle's where life begins!

The Stillness in Between

In the pause, the silence hums,
Amidst the chaos, a laughter comes.
Waiting for wisdom, but what a show,
Tick-tock tickles as answers flow.

The space between thoughts can be funny,
Like a bunny wearing a hat, all sunny.
Jokes that erupt without a cue,
In the still air, there's plenty to skew.

Every moment, a riddle to crack,
With punchlines hidden in the flack.
So here I sit, on this quiet peak,
Tickling time, while I stay meek.

I'll relish the quiet, the skits that bloom,
In the stillness here, I'll give doubts room.
For the comedy dances in questions asked,
And clarity, dear friend, is just a funny mask!

The Threshing Floor of Possibility

In a field of dreams I stand,
Hoping for the bread of truth,
With wheat and chaff, I wave my hand,
Tossed by fate, it's just aloof.

The wind it blows, my hat flies high,
Like opportunities, they soar,
I chase that hat, oh me, oh my,
But clarity? It's just a chore.

A scarecrow nods, a knowing grin,
He's got it all figured out, I swear,
But every time I ask him, when?
He's just a string of silence there.

So here I dance in fields of gold,
With grains of hope and jest of fate,
I pull the stalks, the stories told,
Yet still, I'm left to speculate.

Shadows Whispering Secrets of Tomorrow

In the shadows, secrets creep,
Giggling like kids at the fair,
Tomorrow's tomfooleries sweep,
While I get tangled in my chair.

The clock ticks loud, but time's a prank,
My plans unfold like paper boats,
They sail away, a ceaseless tank,
Of muddy waters and lost quotes.

I eavesdrop on the whispers low,
They giggle like they won't be caught,
They tease me so, these things they know,
Yet nary a clue of what I've sought.

So I pour tea and sip my fate,
With shadows teasing behind the screen,
They laugh and twirl, they love to wait,
For clarity, oh where have you been?

Whispers in the Fog

In the fog, my thoughts collide,
Like one-liners at a stand-up show,
They teeter, tumble, cannot hide,
Playing tag with the winds that blow.

I squint at shapes that dance and sway,
Are they ghosts or just my dreams?
They giggle soft, then slip away,
Turning into nonsense schemes.

A solitary lamp post sighs,
It tries to shed some light on me,
But even it with all its tries,
Can't discern the points of clarity.

So I stumble through the misty blur,
Where laughter echoes, faint yet clear,
I'll hug the humor, that's for sure,
As I wait for answers to appear.

The Horizon Beckons

Across the waves, a line so thin,
The horizon waves, a cheeky tease,
It beckons like a silly grin,
But hides the truth behind the trees.

I squint and search for signs of life,
The seagulls caw, they laugh and glide,
But clarity's a wily wife,
Who dances just beyond my stride.

"Follow me!" she seems to say,
Yet every path leads off the map,
I step with care, and trip on play,
In this comedic little trap.

So here I stand, a hopeful fool,
As ocean whispers tales of grand,
I'll chase the sun, break every rule,
While horizons laugh at my demands.

Whispers of the Unwritten

In a café with a crumpled napkin,
Ideas dance and do the chicken,
A teacup teeters, spills my brew,
   Was it brilliance or just a boo?

A squirrel outside reads my mind,
In acorn sock puppets — so unrefined,
I ponder scripts of the cosmic play,
   Yet can't recall my lunch today.

The waiter winks, my order's wrong,
He serves me fish while I crave prong,
Between the laughs and hiccuped sighs,
   Clarity prances, then quickly flies.

So I scribble down nonsensical lines,
Hoping for truth that whimsically shines,
In the world of jests where dreams collide,
   I'll find the gold inside the fried.

Migrating Clouds of Thought

Like clouds that wander, fluff and sway,
My thoughts jet off on holiday,
They take the bus to places unseen,
While I'm stuck here, caught in between.

A pigeon coos a playful tune,
While I argue with my favorite spoon,
"Is cereal soup?" I muse aloud,
The clouds giggle with a feathery crowd.

The sun peeks through my window pane,
And fills my head with yoga strain,
I twist and turn, still never sure,
If clarity comes with a 'Who's that girl?'

Yet in the chaos, smiles confound,
With every mental fog, there's joy found,
So I'll chase those clouds with a quirky glee,
And let them guide this wandering me.

Lanterns in the Abyss

In the closet of forgotten things,
I find old shoes and question things,
Like why was I hoarding rubber bands?
Clarity hides, slips through my hands.

A haunted lamp with flickering light,
Cast shadows that give me a fright,
It whispers tales of socks astray,
And where that other spoon went to play.

Ghosts of past dinners swirl around,
Chasing memories with a silly sound,
I laugh as I trip over a chair,
Clarity's trailing — she doesn't care.

But in this dungeon, where secrets twinkle,
I gather treasures that make me crinkle,
With every ouch and every jest,
The lanterns glow, I'm feeling blessed.

Navigating the Grey

In the vast sea of fifty shades,
I sail on thoughts that break like waves,
Navigating murky waters deep,
Where certainty likes to take a leap.

A fish on board sings off-key tunes,
While I juggle doubts like rubber balloons,
The compass spins a tale of cheer,
As I ponder what's ahead — or rear.

Mermaids giggle, toss seaweed my way,
"Clarity's lost, come join the play!"
I dive in waves of color and sound,
Finding humor where answers are drowned.

So, with a wink and a playful sigh,
I'll ride the current, wave bye-bye,
To all my cares, as I float and sway,
In the grey sea of 'What do you say?'

Threads of Unraveled Time

In the weave of days, I often tread,
Lost in the patterns spun in my head.
The clock ticks slow, then rushes away,
Like socks in the dryer that won't come to stay.

Thoughts wander off like cats in the night,
Chasing their tails, oh what a sight!
A dance in the haze, a shuffle of shoes,
Finding lost socks and pondering clues.

With each tick-tock, the coffee gets cold,
Stirring my mug, with stories retold.
Yet every missed moment, a laugh in disguise,
Life's tangled yarn leads to surprise.

So hold tight your threads, let them dangle and sway,
For silly mishaps can brighten the day.
In this grand tapestry, the fun never ends,
Where clarity's lost but the laughter transcends.

Echoes in the Fog

In the morning mist, I squint my eyes,
Searching for answers in all the lies.
The street signs dance like they know my plight,
"Turn left at confusion," they wink with delight.

I wander through life, a wandering fool,
Where things have a way of bending the rule.
With each foggy turn, I trip on a grin,
Finding joy in the chaos and glee within.

Conversations happen with shadows and air,
Wondering if they even know I'm there.
The jokes that they tell, oh, how absurd,
Like trying to decipher the noise of a bird.

So I'll keep on strolling through this murky haze,
With laughter my guide on these twisty pathways.
For clarity might be a mythical quest,
But let's have a chuckle; it's truly the best.

Searchlight on the Horizon

I peek through the blinds, a quest on my mind,
Hoping for answers, but clarity's blind.
The searchlight of hope flickers dim in the night,
Like fitting a square peg in wrong, what a fright!

I shout to the stars, "Can you hear me up there?"
Their twinkling replies are just cosmic flair.
A compass that spins, I'm dizzy with glee,
On a treasure hunt for some clarity.

With maps mismatched and directions all wrong,
I find myself humming an off-key song.
But every misstep just adds to the laugh,
Where the journey's the punchline, not the epitaph.

So here's to adventures, however unclear,
With each twist and turn, there's nothing to fear.
For the searchlight will guide me, in its quirky way,
To a land of hilarity, come what may.

Moments Suspended in Air

I throw my thoughts up like balloons in the sky,
Watching them wobble and float by and by.
Each tethered to worry, but some dance so free,
A circus of moments just waiting for me.

I leap from the ground with a grin on my face,
Chasing my dreams in a slapstick race.
Gravity giggles, it pulls me back down,
Yet here I am laughing, lost in this town.

With pockets of time that I've saved for a snack,
I munch on the seconds, what a tasty track!
Each bite flavored sweet with a hint of the wild,
Reliving the fun of each young-hearted child.

So here's to the moments that hover and sway,
In the magic of now, I'll forever stay.
For though I may flounder in disheveled flair,
I'll revel in laughter, in this light-filled air.

Between Breath and Belief

In a world where socks wear out,
I ponder missing pens with doubt.
My coffee's cold, yet dreams are hot,
Two spoons of sugar—you've forgot!

The fridge hums tunes I can't quite place,
What's that smell? Oh no, my grace.
I dance with shadows, not so bright,
Hoping they'll give me a clue tonight.

I chase the cat—a traitor bold,
She mocks my hopes, or so I'm told.
The clock ticks loud, yet time stands still,
A rollercoaster without the thrill.

Yet here I sit, with pie in hand,
Wondering where my plans have planned.
Between each breath, I lose the thread,
Just laughing still, as dreams mislead.

The Dance of Half-Truths

Woke up today with socks that clash,
Consulted Google—made a splash.
The mirror grimaced back at me,
A pirate's life? I'll wait and see.

Half-truths whirling in a twist,
Promises made, but not with fists.
I trip on wisdom, old and gray,
While squirrels hold meetings on display.

Calendar's mockery in plain view,
Lost track of weeks, don't know what's due.
"Trust the process!" they shout and scream,
But I'm still caught in someone's meme.

Yet I'll twirl in mismatched shoes,
Craving knowledge, but not the blues.
In this dance of awkward flair,
I wait for clarity—oh, to dare!

Unraveled by Dawn

The sun spills out with coffee stains,
I fumble through my mental gains.
A sock's elusive, where's its mate?
Why is my plant still on a fate?

The toast is burnt, as usual here,
Flaming hopes in crumbly cheer.
I count the minutes, lost in thought,
And wonder why I'm still distraught.

The morning news is just a joke,
Replaying lives in disarray woke.
Yet, a butterfly flits into view,
Irony sips on morning dew.

So let the day unravel me,
A tapestry of chaos, free!
In this circus, I will reside,
With laughter as my trusty guide.

Stirrings in the Unknown

The fridge hums like it's deep in thought,
What food fights? Oh, I have forgot.
In my head, ideas jiggle and sway,
Like jello on a summer's day.

Tickle the clock as it mocks my hour,
A garden of weeds needs some flower power.
I chase distractions like a kid,
While plans get tangled, as they often did.

In the park, pigeons strut with pride,
They seem to know more, none could hide.
I throw them crumbs, they laugh in glee,
"Please clarify!" I plead, not me.

Yet I shall dust off my best shoe,
Find giggles hidden in despair, too.
With every twist, I'll carve my throne,
In the stirrings of the unknown.

Fragments of a Dream Yet Woven

In a world of socks unmatched,
I search for sense, yet I'm detached.
The coffee spills, the laughter flows,
Yet clarity hides under my toes.

Between my thoughts, a jigsaw plays,
Each piece a riddle, lost in the haze.
I chase the cat, it's on a spree,
Is it chasing dreams, or just me?

In every corner, a whisper calls,
Yet reason ducks and laughter sprawls.
I chew on questions, a bubblegum wand,
Pop! And another thought is gone.

So here I sit, on this jumbled page,
With mismatched socks and a joyful rage.
In fragments bright, my dreams delay,
Yet somehow, they color my day.

The Colors in Between

In shades of gray, I paint the day,
A brush of whimsy, come what may.
A dance of thoughts in colors bold,
Yet meaning hides, some wonders unfold.

Yellow smiles and bluebird sighs,
Polka dots dance, as reality flies.
A canvas sprawled with giggles untold,
In every streak, a tale unfolds.

Between the hues of joy and dread,
Are crudely drawn stick figures instead.
Sharing secrets in a silly muse,
With rainbow dreams that I may choose.

So dip your brush, come paint with me,
In chaotic strokes we'll set minds free.
In every shade, let laughter reign,
For clarity might just be a game.

Sifting Through the Sand of Time

With a bucket and spade, I dig for truth,
But all I find is my lost youth.
Grains slip through fingers, the hourglass grins,
As I build my castles, I trip on sins.

Time ticks softly, a jester's play,
Where moments dance, then slip away.
Tidal waves of yesterday's sand,
Hide treasures tangled in mystery's hand.

I toss a shell into the breeze,
For every wish, there's a twist and tease.
Between each laugh, a tear may droop,
As I watch the clock play hopscotch and loop.

Yet here I giggle at every fail,
As the tide pulls back, I laugh and wail.
In the grains of time, absurdity clings,
While I search for sense in all these flings.

Uncertainty's Woven Tapestry

In threads of chaos, I stitch my fate,
With patterns twisted, I contemplate.
Laughter lingers in the tangled yarn,
As I weave my dreams with hope and scorn.

A poke here, a prod there, what will it be?
Guessing games in absurdity's spree.
Knots and loops that refuse to part,
Are they designs or quirks of the heart?

In the fabric worn, a patchwork hue,
Each stitch sings of fears and joys anew.
What's hiding under this shoddy seam?
Is it clarity or another dream?

I stretch my canvas, absurdly wide,
As uncertainty sways like a confetti tide.
Each woven thread tells a funny tale,
In a tapestry bright where oddness prevails.

Floating in the Space of Maybe

In the cosmos of my doubts, I float,
Juggling dreams like a clown on a boat.
Stars twinkle with secrets just out of reach,
While my brain gives a stand-up comedy speech.

Gravity? I forgot to pay the bill,
So here I am, just going for a thrill.
My thoughts spin like planets in a dance,
Waiting for clarity to take a chance.

Should I steer towards the asteroid belt?
Or coast on clouds where absurdity's felt?
Navigating through a cartoonish haze,
Wishing for a map in this cosmic maze.

Perhaps I'll find answers drawn in the stars,
Or trip over puddles beneath my guitars.
As I float in this space of unpredictable fun,
Who knew being lost could outshine the sun?

Glistening Hopes on the Edge

On the edge of my seat, I sit with a snack,
Nibbling on dreams that might give me a whack.
Hopes glisten bright with each cheerful bite,
As I ponder whether wrong is actually right.

The world spins in circles, like a whirling dervish,
I try to focus; it's making me nervous.
Should I leap into tomorrow, face-first in the cake?
Or just chill on the edge and take a little break?

Every little giggle spills into the night,
While I wonder if I'll be alright.
Life's a circus, no ringmaster here,
But I keep laughing, despite my sheer fear.

On the edge, I tiptoe, looking for signs,
Glistening hopes that dance on the lines.
I reach for the stars, but find only crumbs,
Still, I giggle at life and all its silly hums.

Veils of Anticipation

Behind curtains of hope, I peek and I pry,
Wondering why the snacks always run dry.
Expectation hangs on a thin silver thread,
Like a cat with a laser, insane in its head.

The future waves, then plays a quick game,
Hiding in shadows, it dons a new name.
I chase after clarity, but it's slippery soap,
Sliding through fingers just like my last hope.

Every tick of the clock makes me giggle and sigh,
As I ponder the why's and luck's fishy pie.
Veils of confusion hang low like a mist,
While I wait for that moment when I'll get the gist.

A riddle wrapped tightly in laughter and cheer,
I juggle my thoughts, but none seem clear.
Yet, I sip on uncertainty, oh what a delight,
As veils of anticipation swirl through the night.

The Path Less Lit

On a path less lit, I wander with glee,
Bumping into mysteries and wonders for free.
Twinkles of laughter light every twist,
Though clarity seems like a long-lost sister.

Lost in a fog with a map upside down,
I search for wisdom in this kooky town.
Should I follow the signs or dance in the rain?
Maybe I'll solve it, or maybe I'll just entertain.

Skipping through puddles of existential dread,
I trip over feelings that swirl in my head.
The scenery changes, but I stay the same,
Playing charades in this hilarious game.

Each step is a punchline waiting to land,
As I navigate chaos with twinkling hands.
On the path less lit, where oddities meet,
I find joy in the journey, and make it sweet.

Navigating Through the Mist

Fog rolls in like a sneaky thief,
Hiding plans, causing comic grief.
Lost my glasses, where's the door?
Tripped on a cat, oh, what a score!

Coffee's cold, but it's not too late,
To dance a jig or contemplate.
Socks don't match, I laugh out loud,
In this fog, I'm feeling proud!

Laughter echoes through the haze,
Every mishap a funny phase.
I'm a ship, but where's the shore?
Navigating life's a grand encore!

Muddled thoughts on a drifting breeze,
Should I bother? Should I seize?
With a grin, I forge ahead,
Embracing chaos like it's bread!

Reflections on a Shimmering Surface

Puddles gleam like crystal balls,
I ponder deep as daylight falls.
But a duck quacks – it's quite absurd,
My thoughts are fleeting, just like birds.

Mirror, mirror, don't be shy,
Why do you make my hair ask why?
Shimmering truths, oh where've they gone?
Is honesty just a con?

I see my reflection, pulling a face,
It's the funniest sight in this muddy place.
Do I laugh? Do I blush?
What's the secret? Can I trust this hush?

That old joke about the looking glass,
With every twist, I'm such a gas.
Life's a joke, a riddle square,
Finding clarity? Not a prayer!

The Interval Between Heartbeats

In the silence, a tiny pause,
Thoughts scatter like confetti's cause.
Breathe in, breathe out, now what's the plan?
Oh look, a fly! I'll chase it, man!

Tick-tock kind of jokes unfold,
Whispers in the dark, stories told.
The world spins, my head's in a whirl,
Do I laugh or fully twirl?

Heartbeat races, or is it slow?
Guess I'll dance with a marshmallow.
Every second's a slice of pie,
Too sweet to eat, oh me, oh my!

Between the beats, absurdities blend,
More laughter, more antics to lend.
So here I stand, a jester's hat,
Living these moments - how silly is that!

Searching for the Key in Rusted Locks

Jingling keys, oh what a sound,
But where's the door? It's not around!
Rusted locks, a funny twist,
Why does clarity feel like mist?

I poke and prod all through the day,
To find the lock - and hey, what's play?
Keys stick out, but doors won't budge,
I giggle softly, let's not judge!

A treasure map, drawn by a child,
Leads to nowhere, yet I'm still wild.
I'm searching for sense in all the screws,
A chuckle's the key to shake off blues!

With every turn, my hopes collide,
But laughter starts a wobbly glide.
Irony's charm in every break,
Finding joy is the key I make!

Glimmers of Tomorrow's Light

In the fridge, a rubber chicken,
Dancing dreams and fridge lights flicking.
I ponder deep, like apples in pies,
While my cat gives me judgmental eyes.

The clock ticks slow, a tortoise race,
Chasing hopes in this silly space.
Coffee spills, like visions unclear,
Yet giggles echo, despite the fear.

I'm a jester in a striped coat,
Sailing boats made of old donut floats.
Each hiccup brings a brand new chance,
To trip on nonsense, and sometimes dance.

Tomorrow's glow whispers in dreams,
Between giggles, life bursts at the seams.
Through puddles of doubts, I shall roam,
With a clown nose and a heart as my home.

Standing at the Crossroads of Faith

At the crossroads, where paths collide,
A squirrel debates which nut to hide.
With signs that twist like pretzel sticks,
I laugh out loud; this place just clicks.

Should I turn left for ice cream bliss,
Or right to join a dance-off, amiss?
Juggling choices like a circus pro,
My mind's a carnival, and off I go!

The road is long, a twisty turn,
With each wrong step, new lessons to learn.
Laughter bubbles as I take a leap,
On this crazy ride, no time for sleep.

And if I fall, onto my face,
I'll spring right up, with style and grace.
In this colorful chaos, I confidently sing,
Decisions are silly, let the fun begin!

A Siren's Call Beneath Still Waters

In serene lakes where frogs proclaim,
I search for mermaids, but find just a game.
With a meatball sub as my bait,
I dance with the fish—what a comical fate!

Bubbles rise, with secrets to share,
While ducks quack in synchronized air.
Each splash of humor flips my despair,
Water's a stage, I perform without care.

I hum a tune of jellyfish dreams,
Where giggles float and sunlight beams.
Amidst the waves, bizarre and bright,
Who needs a map? Just follow delight!

But just as I think I've got it all planned,
A wise old turtle offers his hand.
"It's just water, child, don't stop for the fuss,
Swim with laughter, and ride the wild bus!"

The Weight of Unspoken Truths

In a room full of silence, a sock monkey sits,
We share our secrets, with little bits.
I ponder the meaning of yesterday's pie,
As the fridge hums softly, almost a sigh.

Each truth unspoken, like pennies in jars,
Hiding beneath the glow of candy bars.
I trip on my words with dramatic flair,
As the cat rolls her eyes, with a nonchalant air.

A dance of awkwardness, two left feet,
Spinning tales that nobody will tweet.
The weight of the world, or just a bad pun?
I'll lighten the load—let's just have fun!

So here's to the laughter, the giggles, the grins,
Life's bumpy ride, where chaos begins.
When truths get heavy, I'll leap and I'll dance,
With humor as armor, I'll take every chance!

Moments in the Mist

Fog rolls in with a sneaky grin,
I can't see my coffee, where's my din?
Thought I lost my car keys in a twist,
Just my phone in my pocket, what a list!

The cat's a ninja, creeping like a pro,
Even he looks puzzled, moving slow.
Waiting for clarity in every nook,
But here I am lost, it's all just a joke!

My plans are swimming like fish in a stream,
Chasing wild thoughts, I miss the beam.
Where's my roadmap? Oh wait, there's a cat,
Maybe it'll guide me, or just sit and chat!

Dancing with shadows, a waltz in the mist,
Who knew confusion could feel like bliss?
Clarity's out, playing hide and seek,
With every wrong turn, I laugh with glee!

Shadows of Tomorrow

Tomorrow's whispers tease my ear,
I step on shadows but have no fear.
Where's my future? It'll stop for tea,
Or is it stuck in traffic? Oh woe is me!

Plans made in crayon start to smudge,
I wave at hopes, but they won't budge.
A fortune cookie said to chill and bake,
But I can't find the oven for goodness' sake!

Thought I'd get wise with the moon as my guide,
But found my sandwich instead, it just won't hide.
Are dreams a trick or a game of charades?
Because all I feel is caught in the shades!

Twirling in circles like socks in the wash,
Trying to find sense in this strange froth.
But I'll wear my confusion like a badge of cheer,
And laugh at the future, you know, without fear!

Echoes of Uncertainty

Echoes bounce like a yo-yo on strings,
Spinning my thoughts, oh what joy it brings!
Questions like balloons, they float in my head,
Will I catch them all? Or just end up dead?

Riding the wave of a giggle parade,
Life's puzzle pieces all seem to evade.
One cookie says yes, two say 'try again',
But I just want clarity, is that too much to gain?

In a circus of yaks performing ballet,
I try to draw maps that just fade away.
Where are the directions, a GPS cheer?
I ask my pet goldfish, but he just stares here!

Chasing my thoughts like a kid on a swing,
Laughing at chaos, oh what joy it can bring!
In echoes of uncertainty, I choose to play,
For who needs clarity when you're rolling in hay?

The Silence Between Us

There's a thick fog where words can't go,
It's just me and the cat, in quite a show.
We ponder life's puzzles, share our sly looks,
While the world around us is reading the books!

The clock ticks loudly, but is quite unsure,
Am I late for dinner or just wish for more?
A toaster's my therapist, pops out a line,
Was that wisdom baked, or just toast left behind?

In the gaps of silence, I hear loud regret,
Like missing the bus in a giant duet.
We laugh at the echoes, the blunders we make,
Even the kitchen's now joining the shake!

With every pause there's a chuckle to find,
In the silence between us, I'm still quite blind.
But if laughter's the answer, then I won't complain,
I'll toast to confusion, let's do it again!

The Gray Area of Hope

In the shadows of the day,
I sip my tea and say,
Is this the path I seek?
Or just a funny streak?

I wear my shoes untied,
With wobbly steps, I glide.
The world is poking fun,
Have I danced, or just run?

The sky sways and spins,
While my patience thins.
Yet hope's a quirky friend,
With humor that won't end.

So here I stand and wait,
With laughter as my fate.
In gray areas so vast,
I'll find the joy at last.

Seeking the Patterns Within

I search for clues galore,
In socks that bear a score.
Do pairs make sense or not?
Oh, patterns twist and plot!

In the kitchen, pots collide,
And dinner takes a ride.
Recipes turn to jest,
With chaos at its best.

My cats are plotting schemes,
While I chase wobbly dreams.
Patterns might just elude,
But laughter's been my food.

I scribble on the wall,
Sketching patterns, bold and small.
With chaos in full play,
I find joy in the fray.

Ghosts of What Once Was

Old memories knock and sway,
In shadows where I play.
They dance and tease my mind,
With whispers, so unkind.

I trip o'er silly thoughts,
And search for what I've sought.
Ghosts giggle as they swirl,
In this topsy-turvy world.

I call out, 'What are you?'
They snicker, 'Just a few!'
Yet in their ghastly dance,
I find myself in trance.

So let them prance around,
With laughter's joyful sound.
In haunting, I will find,
The humor intertwined.

Mirrors of Possible Futures

I gaze into the glass,
And watch the seconds pass.
Reflections laugh so bright,
As futures hold their light.

Will I trip on my own feet?
Or dance and feel the heat?
Mirrors show me the way,
In all the hues of gray.

With silly grins in tow,
What will tomorrow show?
A mishap or a win,
Shall laughter dwell within?

In futures we entwine,
With humor that will shine.
I'll take my chances here,
For joy is always near.

Flickering Souls in Transit

In the coffee shop line, I'm lost,
Trying to figure what I need most.
A latte or a pastry, what will it be?
Perhaps a side order of existential glee.

My GPS is confused, where's the right lane?
It keeps rerouting me through memory's rain.
A detour for laughter, so I don't feel blue,
And maybe a sign that says, 'This way to you.'

Drifting like clouds in a sky full of jest,
I'm hoping to find where they hide all the best.
Yet every time I think I've got it in view,
It giggles and dances just out of my cue.

So here's to the moments that pad my feet,
The silly mishaps that feel bittersweet.
In this transit of souls, we'll have quite a ride,
As we trip and we tumble, with joy as our guide.

Beyond the Veil of Certainty

Behind every curtain, I peek with delight,
What's hiding there, a cat or a fright?
Is it wisdom or pizza, both smell so divine,
As I trip over questions, just passing the time.

The cosmic jokes played, oh how they amuse,
Like socks in the dryer, which lose all their dues.
I ponder the great, should I wear them in pairs?
Or embrace the absurdity, laughing at stares?

So let's mix up the answers, blend in some cheer,
Forget about meaning, let's just lend an ear.
To the whispers of shadows or socks, who can tell?
Is it nonsense or truth? Oh, it's all just so swell!

With each twist and turn, I'm giggling still,
Chasing down clarity, it waits on the hill.
In a land where the funny goes hand in hand,
I'll tiptoe through riddles, a jester so grand.

Towards an Everlasting Question

Why is there spaghetti on the floor again?
Did I cook up a dream or a whimsical plan?
With meatballs of wonder rolling under my feet,
I wander through choices, so strangely sweet.

Do you taste the questions like a fine cup of tea?
Or dance with the answers, both wild and free?
A riddle wrapped in chaos, a puzzle so grand,
I'll juggle my thoughts, with a clown's steady hand.

So here I am, lost in thoughts that collide,
Does the sun rise for clarity, or just for a ride?
I'll chuckle at time, for it travels so slow,
Like waiting for pizza—when will it show?

Yet in this grand circus, I find my own grace,
Wrestling with questions, a wild, friendly chase.
Each giggle a treasure, each stumble a prize,
As I dance through the chaos, oh how time flies!

Quest of the Unseen

In a world full of wonders, I set out one day,
With a map made of riddles and a compass of play.
Searching for answers in the bottom of a cup,
But all I found was a cat saying, 'What's up?'

Could certainty be hiding behind the next door?
Or is it just another snack I can't ignore?
As I quest through the unseen, a laugh at the weird,
With each silly mishap, my fears disappear.

So many distractions dance along the way,
Like squirrels in a park having their own melee.
I chase after clarity, but what does it mean?
Is it simply the joy of the moments in between?

With every misstep, I find new delight,
In the chaos of not knowing, I twirl through the night.
So here's to the search for the things we can't see,
In this quest of the unseen, I just want to be me!

A Dance of Half-Truths

In the alley of my thoughts, I sway,
With truths like confetti, led astray.
The rhythm's odd, but I still move,
In this quirky dance, I find my groove.

Questions twirl like socks on a line,
While missing answers dodge the sign.
Each step I take, a stumble or glide,
In this masquerade, I take it in stride.

The moon's my partner, ever so bright,
But even it flickers, avoiding the light.
With jiggles of joy, I laugh and jest,
In this half-truth ball, I'm feeling blessed.

So here's to the dance, a muddled affair,
Where clarity prances, but never stays near.
I'll twirl and I'll spin until the day's done,
In this silly charade, I'm having my fun.

The Pause Before the Storm

A stillness blankets my buzzing mind,
Like a cat caught napping, in its own bind.
The clock ticks louder, odd in its phase,
As I sip my tea, lost in a daze.

Clouds pile up with a cheeky smirk,
While I chase shadows, doing the work.
Thunder rumbles like a hungry beast,
And I just want cake—a peculiar feast.

Raincoat on, but I'm still confused,
Is it time for a dance or to feel amused?
I twirl like a leaf, caught in the air,
Not quite a storm, but I'm almost there.

Home's looking cozy, but I'm stuck in limbo,
Waiting for chaos like a distant limbo.
With unexpected laughter, I crack a grin,
In this pause of waiting, my antics begin.

Starlit Doubts and Dimmed Dreams

Under starlit skies, I ponder fair,
With doubts and giggles, dancing in air.
Dreams flicker like fireflies in my head,
While I make up stories to ease my tread.

What if the moon takes a mad detour?
And I'm left waiting for dreams to implore?
While shadows play tricks on my sleepy gaze,
I'm busy counting the stars in a daze.

Each twinkle whispers a tale yet untold,
Of hopes that shimmer, bright but cold.
I slip on my socks, two mismatched pairs,
Laughing at worries that dance in my hairs.

In the vastness of night, I twirl and scheme,
Catching starlit doubts in a whimsical dream.
With chuckles and sighs, I navigate schemes,
Wandering through wonders swathed in my dreams.

Whispers of Unseen Paths

In the forest of choices, branches entwine,
Whispers of futures, both yours and mine.
Each path a riddle, a quirky duet,
With squirrels as guides, I haven't met yet.

I trip on desires, they giggle in glee,
Pointing at options, but none seem to be.
A fork in the road, which way to go?
Safe bets or wild hearts, a game of throw.

With butterflies chuckling, I play the fool,
While chasing the breeze, a whimsical rule.
What if I stumble and find a surprise?
Like rainbows and donuts, in clear blue skies?

So here I wander, through laughter and sighs,
Whispers of choices, like playful spies.
In this maze of moments, I'll take my chance,
With giggles as lanterns, I'll dance my dance.

Traces of What Could Be

In the mirror, I see a face,
Making plans in the wrong place.
I point my finger, scratch my head,
Did I eat that pizza instead?

Dreams on paper, they make me chuckle,
Stuck in thoughts like a bad puzzle.
Hoping for clarity, a shining light,
But tripping on my shoelace feels just right.

A calendar filled, yet I feel bare,
Great ideas but where's the dare?
Pondering life as I take a seat,
Counting socks instead of my beat.

Chasing visions of who I'll be,
While sipping coffee, you know, just me.
Every sip adds to my wait,
Still unsure if I'll be late.

Beneath a Shroud of Time

Clock ticks loudly, but I'm still here,
Lost in thoughts with a hint of fear.
Checking my watch, it's broken too,
Is it lunchtime or past the due?

Time's like jelly, quite spread about,
Waiting for clarity, filled with doubt.
Beneath this shroud, I take a nap,
And dream of skipping the whole trap.

I toss my plans like a salad bowl,
Wondering if they'll ever roll.
Each hour passes in a silly dance,
Should I wear shoes or take a chance?

Watching the clouds as they drift away,
Plotting my future, come what may.
Each tick brings giggles, a funny tune,
What if clarity came with a balloon?

Threads of the Unfolding

Like a sweater with a loose thread,
I pull and tug, what will be said?
Each pull reveals a tangled fate,
But I'd prefer a side of grate.

Here I am, threads all askew,
Trying to weave something anew.
With every stitch, a chuckle grows,
What a mess, yet who really knows?

Laughing at plans that won't quite fit,
Creating a patchwork, bit by bit.
The loom of time keeps twisting tight,
I take a break for a cupcake bite.

Making a riddle of where to go,
Stitching dreams in a comic show.
Oh, clarity, why are you shy?
Guess I'll just laugh and let it fly.

The Space of Hesitation

Between the here and what could be,
    I find myself on another spree.
    Should I jump or just stay put?
    Maybe dance with a silly strut?

In this space, I forget to blink,
Lost in thoughts, I start to sink.
Should I text or go outside?
Decisions made with a chocolate slide.

Every option feels quite bizarre,
Should I drive or just walk far?
Spinning circles with a hefty grin,
    Even hesitation can be a win.

So here I sit with a grin so wide,
Hesitating, but taking it in stride.
Waiting for clarity, what a show,
Maybe tomorrow, I just won't know.

Expressions Yet to Emerge

I woke up in a daze,
Pajamas still on my face.
Coffee brewing like a race,
Yet I'm lost in outer space.

Thoughts tumble, dance, and twirl,
Like socks left in a whirl.
I scribble, giggle, and unfurl,
Each idea a drunken pearl.

My dreams are silly, float like foam,
Chasing snacks, I roam my home.
With every glance, I feel the chrome,
Of thoughts like squirrels, I call them 'Gnome.'

Battles rage with lunch so fair,
Is it toast, or is it air?
With every bite, I pull my hair,
Yet in the end, who really cares?

Lingering at the Crossroads

Two paths sit, both look the same,
One leads to snacks, one to fame.
A fork in time, a silly game,
Where's that map? Am I to blame?

A sign says 'ice cream' to the right,
While left screams 'work' with all its might.
I ponder long; should I take flight,
And try the cone that looks so bright?

Lost in thought, I trip on grass,
Maybe there I'll find my sass.
Or perhaps I'll just let silence pass,
As squirrels laugh and shoot me sass.

Twilight sways like a pendulum,
Dreams as tasty as double gum.
Should I go, or should I run?
Oh, how I wish this stroll was fun!

Wandering Between Seconds

Tick-tock goes the feeble clock,
But who cares if I walk or balk?
Seconds swirl in a wobbly flock,
Each moment's juice a soggy sock.

A squirrel walks by with grand intent,
I guess he's judging where I went.
His tiny paws are heaven-sent,
While my goals seem quite content.

Funny how time just refuses to budge,
I'm stuck here with a peanut fudge.
With every minute, I hold a grudge,
A dance-off with fate—let's not budge!

In this limbo, I chew my pen,
Sketching thoughts of where I've been.
Who knew clarity was a whim?
I laugh at time, no need to swim!

Stories on the Edge of Understanding

Once wrote a tale with no clear end,
Full of twists like a broken bend.
Each character just a silly friend,
In a world where ducks could send!

I ponder plots, my brain's a blob,
With loose threads like a jiggly mob.
Each creative bit's a funny sob,
As I scan the room for a good job.

Missing pieces flutter like leaves,
With every attempt, a laugh it weaves.
No one said that clarity cleaves,
Unscrambling eggs, it's all in sleeves!

So here I am, not much to show,
Just half-formed tales of too much flow.
But gladly here, I laugh and glow,
In confusion's charm, I truly grow.

Conversations with Silence

I asked silence where to go,
It winked and pointed at my shoe.
I tripped over my own two feet,
Silence chuckled, what a view!

I tried to chat with empty air,
It just sat there without a care.
I told a joke, it didn't laugh,
Maybe silence needs some flair.

I pondered deep on what to say,
But silence seemed to shy away.
I offered snacks, a cup of tea,
It frowned, then made me go and play.

So next time you have words to share,
Remember silence really doesn't care.
It's fine with just the quiet hum,
And a mix of giggles in the air.

Maps of the Undefined

I found a map with no clear path,
It led me in a loop of math.
I drew a spot with big red X,
But it just giggled, oh, what a gaffe!

I navigated with a spoon and fork,
Spinning circles, feeling like a dork.
The stars above seemed to just hide,
While I chased shadows for a quirk.

A compass spun with no intent,
Its needle danced, a party sent.
I asked it for a bit of help,
It pointed north to my cement.

So now I wander, maps in hand,
Trying to plot on shifting sand.
Laughing at the twists of fate,
Maybe this chaos is the grand plan.

The Weight of Expectation

I walked a plank of high demand,
With hopes and dreams all close at hand.
The weight of wishes on my back,
Like carrying a marching band.

I reached for stars, they slipped away,
As if they knew I couldn't stay.
I danced instead with fleeting thoughts,
And joked why hopes can't learn to play.

I wore a suit of "should have been,"
All buttoned up, it felt like sin.
I laughed at all the silly rules,
That said I can't just simply grin.

So here I stand, expectations spread,
With dreams piled high up on my head.
A silly hat is all I need,
To keep this funny circus fed.

Moments Adrift

I drifted on a boat of dreams,
With oars made out of soft ice creams.
The winds of doubt blew strong and loud,
While giggles burst at the seams.

A jellyfish held my navigation,
It bobbed along with glee elation.
I winked and waved, it wobbled back,
A true friend in the situation.

Clouds looked down and started to frown,
We laughed aloud, then spun around.
Each splash of joy, a silly cheer,
In these moments, none were drowned.

So here I sip my soda-sweet,
And ride the waves with dancing feet.
Adrift in jokes and silly rhymes,
Each heartbeat shines, oh, what a treat!

When Shadows Play Hide and Seek

In corners where whispers softly creep,
Shadows giggle, secrets they keep.
They dart and dash, a playful game,
While I wonder if I'm quite the same.

Behind the couch and under the chair,
I find them lurking without a care.
They tease and taunt with their sly little grins,
While I'm lost in thoughts where confusion begins.

Through the windows, they leap and sway,
Like jolly dancers in a sunlit ballet.
I chase them down, but they slip away,
"Can someone tell me, is it night or day?"

Eventually, they fade with the light,
And I sit, pondering the absurdity in sight.
Perhaps they know what I do not see,
As I laugh alone, just shadows and me.

Beneath the Veil of Uncertainty

Wrapped in a blanket of fog and doubt,
I squint at the world, wondering about,
Should I wear my glasses or go blind?
The answers may leave me behind.

Choices float like balloons in the air,
One pops, and I'm left with a scare.
I juggle thoughts like a clown at a fair,
Hoping clarity will show it cares.

The magic eight ball sits on the shelf,
It couldn't forecast a sneeze from myself.
"Ask again later," it smugly states,
While I bang my head against the fates.

Yet, in this muddle, I find some glee,
Like a cat chasing shadows, wild and free.
Though paths seem twisted, and some are unclear,
I'll dance through the fog, with laughter and cheer.

In the Quiet of Unanswered Questions

Sitting still, the clock ticks loud,
Each tick a question, bustling a crowd.
"Why do socks vanish in the wash?"
I scratch my head, then slowly nosh.

In the silence, my mind takes flight,
Pondering why it's always night!
Why does my coffee always spill,
When I'm running late? Oh, what a thrill!

A riddle, a puzzle, in my mind it spins,
Is it the universe or just my sins?
Yet I chuckle, plotting my next quest,
To solve the riddles and get some rest.

In this quiet, laughter is my guide,
Finding humor in what I try to hide.
For life's a riddle, funny and bright,
And unanswered questions don't steal my light.

Chasing the Gossamer Dawn

With jellybeans gleaming in morning sun,
I chase the dawn, it's all in good fun.
Like a child with a kite, I leap and twirl,
For gossamer dreams make my heart whirl.

But dawn is shy, it dances away,
Peeking through clouds, then hides all day.
I waved my hands, but no one would stay,
"Oh come on, don't be such a cliché!"

The sky chuckles, "Where did you think you'd go?"
As the colors blush and the breezes flow.
I spin in circles, arms wide like wings,
Chasing the laughter that morning brings.

So here I am, like a merry fool,
In the whims of dawn, I find my rule.
For every chase brings a smile anew,
And the gossamer dawn is worth the hue.

With Every Flicker of Hope

A candle dance on the table,
Its wax is now a sad fable.
The shadows laugh, a silly sight,
As I'm wishing for some light.

The fridge hums of forgotten meals,
Chasing dreams like rubber seals.
My socks have become a wild pair,
Still searching for that comfy chair.

The clock ticks like a sneaky thief,
Its hands are spinning, what a belief!
They say time flies, I beg to differ,
It drips like syrup, makes me quiver.

So here I sit, in this great wait,
With a side of fries upon my plate.
Hope flickers like a caffeine buzz,
In this absurd, yet cozy fuzz.

In the Depths of the Unsaid

Under blankets of unsaid words,
Where silence sings with chirping birds.
I stare at walls, they stare right back,
As thoughts parade in a wobbly stack.

My cat's a sage, who smirks at me,
With her whiskers twitching, so carefree.
She's judging all my deep, grand plans,
While I juggle dreams like madcap clowns.

The laundry piles up, a mountain high,
Yet my mind wanders, oh my, oh my!
Time's a jester, playing tricks,
With hidden meanings and silly mix.

I ponder things, while sipping tea,
Chasing thoughts as they flee from me.
In the abyss of 'what could be',
I chuckle loud, oh, set me free!

Waters Flowing Towards Tomorrow

A river flows, or maybe trickles,
With dreams afloat like silly pickles.
I toss my hopes like paper boats,
But instead, they sink and gloat.

The fish debate my grand designs,
As water plants compose their lines.
I splash around this wobbly quest,
While turtles ponder, 'What's next?'

Time slips through like sand in glass,
I wish it'd slow, not rush, alas!
The frogs croak wisdom from a throne,
While I just want to be left alone.

I cast my nets in gentle streams,
Hoping to catch some silly dreams.
Yet here I wait, a tad confused,
With the current playing, feeling used.

When the Stars Remain Unread

Stars twinkle like they've lost their script,
As I ponder if I've really flipped.
What do they whisper, up so high?
Do they giggle at me, passing by?

I chart my fate with a crayon map,
While the constellations take a nap.
The Big Dipper is in a snooze,
All my wishes get lost in the blues.

Oh universe, can't you see?
I need guidance, maybe tea?
With the moon grinning, I shout aloud,
"Make it clear or I'll join the crowd!"

When the stars lie in their cosmic bed,
I dance around with my thoughts unsaid.
In this confusion, I take my cue,
To laugh it off, a comical view.

Uprising from the Blur

In a haze of socks and spilled tea,
I search for answers beneath my knee.
The cat yawns wide, with a smirk on his face,
While my thoughts drift off, at a slow, steady pace.

The toaster pops, a joke in disguise,
Burnt bread, my breakfast, oh what a surprise!
I shuffle around, like a confused old mime,
Today feels like yesterday, or maybe a crime.

The calendar laughs, it's a comedy show,
Days dance around, but I'm moving too slow.
The mirror's a partner, reflecting my plight,
With a wink and a nod, says, "It'll be all right."

So here's to the puzzles, a riddle or two,
In a world that's askew, I'll just laugh with the view.
With each step I take in this whimsical blur,
Someday I'll figure it out, that's for sure!

In the Realm of Unknowing

In the fridge, the leftovers hold a debate,
A rogue carrot, a wishful plate, oh fate!
Like a TV show, on a loop for a while,
I'm half-heartedly trying, but can't fake a smile.

The clock on the wall ticks a bit offbeat,
Tick-tock, tick-tock, like I'm glued to my seat.
Time's having a party, but I'm not on the list,
An outsider's dance, in a food-fighting mist.

My phone buzzes, a ghost of connection,
Yet all I feel is a mild disconnection.
Texting my pals, for advice or a clue,
They laugh at my struggles, what else can I do?

In this twilight zone, where confusion is king,
I sit and I ponder what tomorrow will bring.
With a giggle and snort, I embrace the unknown,
After all, it's just me, my soup, and my phone.

Hues of a Faded Dream

Colors clash on the palette of thought,
With wild strokes of worry, my canvas is caught.
A rainbow of questions, no answers to find,
Just snickers and giggles as I lose track of time.

In slippers I wander, through shades of the past,
Finding treasures long lost, but they don't seem to last.
Each step feels like art, abstract but shy,
As I search through the chaos, both laughing and dry.

The sun sneezes bright, amid clouds full of cheer,
Chasing shades of uncertainty, year after year.
The hues are a blessing, a colorful mess,
And I can't help but chuckle at this funny distress.

A palette of nonsense, a canvas so wide,
I paint with my laughter, my heart open wide.
With each stroke of humor, this dream fades away,
Ah, but it's all in good fun, come what may!

Tides of Waiting

Here comes the tide as I stand on the shore,
Waves lapping gently, what am I here for?
The sea tells me secrets, or is it just wind?
With each crashing wave, new questions rescind.

I draw in the sand, a mural of doubt,
"Why's my lunch colder than a winter without?"
Seagulls laugh loudly, they circle above,
While I'm arrested by uncertainty and love.

A shell in my pocket, a heart in my hand,
The tide rolls on, but I can barely stand.
Each ebb of the ocean says, "Maybe, just maybe,"
I'll catch the next wave, feeling light and quite crazy.

So I'm surfing this wait, on my whimsical board,
Dancing with laughter, by the sea I'm adored.
In the currents of fate, with a wink at the sun,
I embrace all the breezes, oh, this waiting is fun!

www.ingramcontent.com/pod-product-compliance
Lightning Source LLC
Chambersburg PA
CBHW072144200426
43209CB00051B/385